Living
Shojin
Ryori

Danny Chu

Living Shojin Ryori

Plant-based Cooking from the Heart

Marshall Cavendish
Cuisine

Instagram: @gobo_tabbycat

To my gurus, 14th Dalai Lama Tenzin Gyatso, Drukpa Choegon Rinpoche, Lama Zopa Rinpoche, Lama Lhundrup and Geshe Chonyi, who have shown me great compassion and wisdom through their enlightened activities and teachings. Their blessings made all things possible.

In memory of my mum, Nancy, and my partner, Diamond — your love made me believe that dreams really, and do, come true. You will always be in my heart.

To my tabby cat, Gobo, who purrs me on till today.

About the Author

Danny Chu is a former foreign currency trader who left the corporate world and followed his passion to Japan to learn more about *shojin ryori*, the art of Japanese Zen cuisine. With hard work and unwavering determination, Danny mastered traditional Zen temple cooking and became the first *shojin ryori* chef in Singapore.

He ran Enso Kitchen for several years, delighting both vegetarians and non-vegetarians alike with his creative dishes, and garnered rave reviews from the media, including *Wine & Dine*, *Travel+Leisure*, *BBC Good Food*, *Appetite* and *The Peak* magazines, as well as *The Business Times* and Channel News Asia.

Danny's first cookbook, *Shojin Ryori: The Art of Japanese Vegetarian Cuisine*, won Best Japanese Cuisine Book (Best in the World category) in the 2015 Gourmand World Cookbook Awards. A new edition of the book is now available as *Shojin Ryori: Mindful Japanese Vegetarian Cooking*.

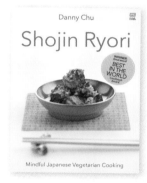

Currently based in Taiwan, Danny shares his love for *shojin* cooking through classes and demonstrations overseas.

Contents

Introduction

Shojin ryori is a traditional vegetarian cuisine that originated from Buddhist temples in Japan. The monks in the temples incorporate the philosophies and the processes of *shojin* cooking in their daily practices to achieve a mental state of peace and tranquility. As such, *shojin ryori* is sometimes translated as 'food of devotion'.

This aspect of Zen training requires one to observe abstention from meat, fish, egg and dairy products, which makes *shojin ryori* a vegan-friendly diet. Its simple recipes and careful cooking processes allow cooking at home to be a mindful practice and life's simplicity and goodness to be enjoyed. In *shojin ryori*, less is indeed more.

The main essence of *shojin* cooking is to use ingredients by the seasons, to extract the best flavours and optimum nutrition. All ingredients used are pure, whole vegetables or obtained from plant sources. Typical ingredients used include seasonal vegetables, dried foodstuffs such as seaweed, mushrooms and tofu products, and the main seasonings include salt, soy sauce, mirin and miso.

Much attention is placed on the presentation of a *shojin* meal setting where a variety of dishes are prepared, as much as possible, to offer different flavours (sweet, sour, bitter, salty and savoury) and multiple colours (red, yellow, green, white and black) and cooking styles. Artificial colourings and flavourings, as well as onions, garlic, scallions, chives and leeks, are avoided.

Shojin ryori cooks also make sure not to waste any of the ingredients; Zen practitioners try to eat all of the food prepared during the day, and throw nothing edible away. It is also customary in Zen temples to chant five reflections before eating:

The effort that brought me this meal
This is an appreciation of the effort made to put the meal together, from harvesting the crops to preparing the ingredients and even those who made the tableware and cutlery. The meal is possible only through the kindness of others.

My imperfections as I receive this meal

This is the recognition that nobody is perfect, so the individual is kept humble and the heart open, thankful and appreciative of the goodness of life.

Mindfulness to be free from imperfections

This is to keep free from negativity through rightful actions, speech and thinking. Only when one is fully aware of his shortcomings, would he seek to change for the better.

Taking this food to sustain good health

The essence of this reflection is to be mindful of what one eats as food has an impact on health.

The fulfillment of our obligations

The essence of living is to achieve one's goals. With this in mind, the individual is able to uplift his spirits and reach his goals.

Like in traditional Chinese medicine, the way a *shojin* meal is prepared — focused on colours, tastes, cooking styles and the seasons — is associated with the five main elements in nature. The five elements are wood (spring), fire (summer), earth (late summer), metal (autumn) and water (winter). Through the process of cooking and eating a *shojin* meal, one will be able to achieve a balance within oneself and also attain harmony with nature.

Shojin ryori is more than just food that we consume to satisfy our appetite. Another aspect of cooking by seasons is to instill mindfulness that brings our focus to the present moment. It helps us appreciate certain characteristics of the seasons and its associated elements, and relate it to our daily life. This nourishes us physically, mentally, emotionally and spiritually.

For instance, spring is represented by the element of wood, and is when leaves start to sprout. Trees grow in the direction of the sun and its branches snap easily if they are too brittle. This metaphor reinforces the importance of being decisive yet maintaining a sense of flexibility when reaching after goals.

Summer, being the hottest season, is associated with fire. Days are brightened by many colourful flowers and vegetables. This encourages us to follow our passion and reminds us that whatever we do should always give us a sense of joy.

With late summer, nature returns the fruits it has made, which are ripe and ready to be picked. We associate late summer with the element, earth. Fruits are harvested and conserved so that we can survive autumn and winter without scarcity. This reminds us to adopt a down-to-earth approach in life.

Autumn is known to be the most picturesque season with falling leaves. It is as if someone is using metal knives to prune the trees and thus explains the association with the element of metal. The sight of falling leaves in autumn suggests we should always remember to let go and lighten our burdens.

Winter, being the coldest season, is inevitably associated with the water element. Animals and plants go into hibernation, reminding us to find time to relax and rejuvenate ourselves by going for a retreat or on a vacation.

As *shojin ryori* is an art, it allows us flexibility to be creative and discover new recipes, lessons and philosophies. I find it fruitful to keep an open mind and learn from nature. The rules and philosophies should not be a constraint or burden.

I have written the recipes inspired by the seasons – Spring, Summer, Autumn, Winter and All Seasons – and also included individual sections showing Soups, Pickles and Desserts. It is perfectly fine to cook them individually without serving them as a set. If you like to cook *shojin ryori* meals by preparing different dishes and serving them together based on the seasons, you can take a look at some of the suggestions in my first cookbook, *Shojin Ryori: Mindful Japanese Vegetarian Cooking*. The dishes found there can be substituted with those featured in this cookbook.

The next time when you prepare *shojin ryori*, use seasonal ingredients as much as possible and develop your awareness of the season and the gifts it brings. I hope you enjoy this cookbook and the recipes. *Itadakimasu* with folded hands.

Basic Preparations

In this section are several basic recipes, such as stocks, batter and garnishes, that are used for the dishes in this cookbook. They will also be useful for Japanese cooking in general.

You do not need any sophisticated kitchen tools to prepare *shojin ryori*. A customer who spent a lot on kitchen tools and equipment was very surprised that I didn't even have an oven in my kitchen. Nevertheless, you should use anything to make your job in the kitchen easier.

KONBU DASHI

Makes 1.25 litres (40 fl oz)

12-cm (5-in) konbu

1.25 litres (40 fl oz) water

Wipe the surface of konbu with a clean damp cloth. Soak in a pot of water for at least 2 hours.

Bring the water to the boil. Lower heat and simmer for 10 minutes.

Remove konbu. The konbu dashi is ready to be used.

If you cannot afford the time to soak konbu for 2 hours, a faster way is to go straight to the second step and simmer for 20 minutes.

In *shojin* cooking, konbu dashi is a main stock that uses only konbu for soup bases. Unlike most Japanese cooking, *bonito* (fish flakes) are not added.

MUSHROOM DASHI and RECONSTITUTED DRIED MUSHROOMS

Makes 1.25 litres (40 fl oz)

8 dried shiitake mushrooms

1.25 litres (40 fl oz) water

Rinse mushrooms and soak in a pot of water for at least 3 hours.

Remove mushrooms and gently squeeze the water back into the pot.

The mushroom dashi and reconstituted dried mushrooms are ready to be used.

If there is no time to soak mushrooms for 3 hours, a quick way is to place the mushrooms in a pot of water. Bring it to the boil. Lower heat and simmer for 10-15 minutes. Remove mushrooms and set aside. When cool, gently squeeze the water into the pot. The mushroom dashi and reconstituted dried mushrooms are ready to be used.

TEMPURA BATTER

120 g (4¹/₂ oz) plain (all-purpose) flour

130 ml (4 fl oz) water

Sea salt, as needed

In a bowl, combine flour and water and mix well.

Then add salt as needed.

If the batter is too thick, add more water (a little at a time). If it is too thin, add more flour.

Do not use hot water.

If you are not using the batter immediately, you should stir and mix well again before deep frying.

You can use drops of the batter to test if the oil is hot enough for deep frying. You should see bubbling and the batter droplets floating to the surface almost immediately. Make sure there is not too much smoke — that means the oil is too hot.

GRATED GINGER

10 g (¹/₃ oz) knob ginger

Scrap off the skin of the ginger using a metal tea spoon.

Using an *oroshigane* (Japanese-style grater), finely grate the ginger.

If the juice and the pulp need to be used separately, you can gently press through a fine sieve.

An *oroshigane* (Japanese-style grater) is different from the usual American-style grater. With a Japanese grater, the grated material stays on top unlike with an American-style grater, where the grated material falls through holes.

As a general guide, 10 g (¹/₃ oz) of knob ginger makes 1 tsp of ginger juice and 20 g (²/₃ oz) of knob ginger makes 1 Tbsp of ginger juice.

Spring

With the arrival of spring, associated with
the element of wood, nature resumes its vitality.
Leaves sprout, flowers blossom and trees lean towards
the sun. Yet branches snap easily if they are brittle,
so the season of spring is the season of possibilities
and growth, strength and suppleness.

SPINACH with PEANUT DRESSING

Serves 4

200 g (7 oz) spinach

$^1/_2$ tsp sea salt

1 tsp raw sugar

PEANUT DRESSING

4 Tbsp chopped roasted peanuts

4 Tbsp Japanese soy sauce

4 tsp sake

4 tsp raw sugar

Using a *surikogi* (pestle), finely grind the peanuts in the *suribachi* (mortar). Add soy sauce, sake and sugar and mix well.

Rinse spinach and trim off the roots. Boil a pot of water and add salt and sugar. Blanch spinach for about 1 minute, then remove and rinse in cold water. Drain and squeeze gently to remove water. Cut lengthwise into equal portions.

Place boiled spinach on 4 individual serving plates and serve with the peanut dressing.

Substitute spinach with any leafy vegetable.

Salt and sugar are added to boiling water when blanching leafy greens to obtain a bright green colour.

Instead of the more typically used sesame seeds, this recipe uses aromatic roasted peanuts. Other nuts such as walnuts and almonds, or a combination of different nuts, can also be used to make the dressing.

SPINACH YUBA MAKI

Serves 4

250 g (9 oz) spinach

4 fresh *yuba* sheets

1 Tbsp black sesame seeds

MISO SAUCE

2 Tbsp sweet miso

1 Tbsp peanut butter
(unsweetened)

1 Tbsp raw sugar

1 Tbsp sake

Mix all the ingredients for the miso sauce in a saucepan over low heat. Turn off heat when sugar is dissolved. Set aside.

Rinse spinach leaves well and trim off crowns.

Boil a pot of water and add salt and sugar. Add spinach and parboil for about 1 minute. Remove and rinse in cold water. Drain and gently squeeze to remove any excess water. Portion out into 4 bundles.

Place a fresh *yuba* sheet on chopping board and arrange a bundle of spinach across, lengthwise, at one end. Roll up the *yuba* sheet and firmly squeeze to shape into a solid round roll. Cut into desired number of pieces (preferably lengths of 2–3 cm). Repeat for the other 3 *yuba* sheets and spinach bundles.

Arrange on 4 individual serving plates. Sprinkle some black sesame seeds over and serve with miso sauce.

Substitute fresh *yuba* with dried yuba sheets which may be more easily available. Reconstitute by soaking in water for 30 seconds or until soft, then pat dry.

If there is no *yuba* available, use nori seaweed.

Parboiled spinach should be squeezed dry without retaining too much water.

Yuba is a by-product of soy milk that is often used in *shojin* cooking. This is a unique alternative to typical *maki* (sushi rolls) using fresh *yuba* skin and spinach, which is both delicate and refreshing.

SHUNGIKU and DAIKON with SESAME DRESSING

Serves 4

50 g (1³/₄ oz) *shungiku* (chrysanthemum) leaves

3-cm (1¹/₂-in) length daikon

¹/₂ tsp rice

1 tsp sesame oil

1 Tbsp Japanese soy sauce

SESAME DRESSING

1 Tbsp sesame paste

1 Tbsp Japanese soy sauce

1 Tbsp sake

1 tsp rice vinegar

1 Tbsp raw sugar

To prepare the sesame dressing, add all the ingredients in a bowl and mix well.

Rinse *shungiku* leaves and drain dry. Remove thick stems and discard. Chop the leafy parts into bite-sized pieces.

Peel and cut daikon into bite-size wedges of 0.5 cm (¹/₄ in) thick.

Boil a pot of water and add daikon and rice. Simmer for about 20 minutes or until daikon is tender. Remove and drain well.

Heat sesame oil in a pan. Add boiled daikon and cook until the pieces are a little charred around the edges. Add soy sauce and cook for another 1 minute.

Place *shungiku* and daikon on 4 individual serving plates, spoon the sesame dressing over and serve.

Substitute *shungiku* with any salad greens and daikon with apple to make a raw salad dish.

The distinct aroma of *shungiku* leaves is akin to the incense that is burnt in temples to purify the meditation room. The crunchy daikon gives body to this simple side dish.

BEETROOT with HIJIKI

Serves 4

10 g (¹/₃ oz) dried *hijiki*

150 ml (5 fl oz) apple juice

160 g (5¹/₂ oz) beetroot

1 tsp sesame oil

1 tsp Japanese soy sauce

1 Tbsp raw sugar

Sea salt, as needed

Rinse the *hijiki* and soak in apple juice for 30 minutes. Discard apple juice and drain well.

Peel and grate beetroot.

Heat sesame oil in a pan. Add grated beetroot, soy sauce, sugar and salt and sauté for about 10 minutes.

Add *hijiki* and sauté for another 3 minutes.

Divide into 4 equal portions on individual serving plates and serve.

Choose hard and firm beetroots. Smaller ones are sweeter.

Both beetroot and *hijiki* have exceptional nutritional value. However, their strong, distinct aromas may not appeal to some. This simple recipe tones down the flavours, allowing more people to enjoy and benefit from these two superfoods.

ASPARAGUS with YURINE

Serves 4

1-2 fresh *yurine* (lily bulb)

12 large green asparagus spears

100 ml (3¹/₃ fl oz) konbu dashi (page 16)

1 Tbsp Japanese soy sauce

1 Tbsp sake

Sea salt, as needed

Wash *yurine* and trim the base. Remove any black spots and steam the *yurine* petals for about 10 minutes or until soft. Set aside to cool.

Trim root ends of asparagus and cut into halves or thirds lengthwise.

Heat konbu dashi in a pan and add asparagus, soya sauce, sake and salt. Simmer for about 2-3 minutes or until tender.

Add *yurine* and gently stir in. Mix well and mash gently so that the simmering stock becomes a thick, starchy paste. Simmer for another 1-2 minutes.

Divide into 4 equal portions and serve.

Do not overcook asparagus. Overcooking will deplete its flavour.

Most people are surprised to find out that this soft, creamy paste that complements the asparagus so much is actually *yurine* (lily bulb). This is definitely a more unusual cooking method to prepare *yurine* that brings an elegant touch to the dish.

POTATO and SHISO SALAD

Serves 4

150 g (5$\frac{1}{3}$ oz) potato

6 shiso leaves

UMEZUKE DRESSING

1 *umezuke* (pickled plum)

1 tsp Japanese soy sauce

1 Tbsp sake

1 tsp sesame oil

$\frac{1}{4}$ tsp wasabi

Remove the pit from the *umezuke* and crush the flesh, then add sake, soy sauce, sesame oil and wasabi. Mix well and set aside.

Remove and discard stems of the shiso leaves. Chiffonade shiso leaves.

Wash potato thoroughly and julienne. Soak in water for 10-15 minutes and drain well.

Boil a pot of water and add potato sticks. Simmer for about 2-3 minutes. Remove and drain well.

Transfer potato sticks and shiso leaves to a bowl. Add *umezuke* dressing and mix well.

Divide into 4 equal portions on individual serving plates and serve.

....

Do not overcook potato. Overcooking will make it soggy.

You can substitute *umezuke* with pickled apricots.

Shiso leaves come in green or purple.
Its distinctive, vibrant taste adds a refreshing touch
to this salad with a tangy pickled plum
and wasabi dressing.

SIMMERED BAMBOO SHOOTS

Serves 4

250–300 g (9–10 1/2 oz) bamboo shoots

BOILING BAMBOO SHOOTS

1 tsp rice

For every 3 litres (96 fl oz) water, use:

2 Tbsp raw sugar

1 tsp sea salt

SIMMERING STOCK

200 ml (6 2/3 fl oz) konbu dashi (page 16)

1 tsp Japanese soy sauce

1 Tbsp sake

1/2 tsp sea salt

Wash bamboo shoots and place in a pot. Fill water to cover bamboo shoots. Add sugar, salt and rice and bring to a boil. Lower heat and simmer for 1 hour or until tender.

Peel off outer skin of the bamboo shoots and cut into bite-sized wedges.

Prepare konbu dashi in a saucepan. Add soy sauce, sake and salt and bring to a boil. Reduce heat and add bamboo shoot pieces. Simmer for 30 minutes.

Remove bamboo shoot pieces and arrange in 4 shallow bowls. Serve with some broth spooned over.

You can add the boiled bamboo shoot, soy sauce, sake and salt to cook together with rice. When done, fluff and serve as bamboo shoot rice.

Bamboo shoots sprout from the earth in
springtime and are heavy and firm.
Though this recipe requires quite a long cooking time,
it is a versatile dish that can be prepared as a side dish
or cooked together with rice.

GREEN BEANS in PLUM BROTH

Serves 4

130 g (4¹/₂ oz) green beans

SIMMERING STOCK

100 ml (3¹/₃ fl oz) mushroom dashi (page 16)

1 *umezuke* (pickled plum)

1 tsp Japanese soy sauce

1 tsp sake

1 tsp mirin

¹/₂ tsp sesame oil

Trim ends of green beans and cut into 4-cm lengths.

Remove the pit from the *umezuke* and crush the flesh.

In a saucepan, add mushroom dashi, sake, mirin, soy sauce, sesame oil and *umezuke*. Mix well.

Add green beans and cook on medium heat for 1-2 minutes.

Remove beans and arrange on 4 shallow bowls. Serve with some broth spooned over.

. . . .

Substitute green beans with any stocky greens such as asparagus and *warabi* (fiddlehead fern).

A light dish that uses the refreshingly
sour *umezuke* (pickled plum) with added
sesame oil to enrich its flavour. You can use asparagus
or *warabi* (fiddlehead fern), if that is available.

Summer

The season of bright sunshine and colourful produce is associated with fire, creativity and basking in the warmth. Late summer, associated with the element of earth, presents the ripe fruits of nature, ready to be harvested and conserved. This reminds us of our reliance on the earth and inspires gratitude.

OKRA in GINGER BROTH

Serves 4

180 g (6¹/₃ oz) okra
(ladies' fingers)

10 g (¹/₃ oz) grated ginger

250 ml (8 fl oz) mushroom
dashi (page 16)

2 Tbsp Japanese soy sauce

1 Tbsp sake

1 Tbsp mirin

1 tsp sesame oil

¹/₄ tsp sea salt

Wash and trim stem ends of okra.

Place mushroom dashi, soy sauce, sake, mirin, sesame oil and salt in a saucepan and bring to the boil. Lower heat and add okra and grated ginger. Simmer for about 10 minutes.

Remove and arrange on 4 individual serving plates. Serve with some broth spooned over.

. . . .

Cut into halves if you are using okra of longer lengths.

Okra is a superfood popular with the health conscious
as it is high in dietary fibre and low in calories.
This is a quick, easy side dish with ginger added
to perk up tastebuds in the summer.

TOMATO with GRATED DAIKON

Serves 4

120 g (4 oz) tomato

120 g (4 oz) daikon

1 Tbsp mirin

1 tsp sake

1½ Tbsp maple syrup

¼ tsp sea salt

Make crisscross cut at the base of each tomato. Boil a pot of water and blanch tomato briefly, about 30 seconds. Transfer to a bowl of ice water. When cooled, remove the skin. Core and seed tomato and dice into small pieces.

Peel and finely grate daikon. Lightly squeeze out excess water from daikon - it should still be very moist but not drip without pressing.

Place daikon in a bowl and mix well with tomato, mirin, sake, maple syrup and salt.

Divide into 4 equal portions on individual serving plates and serve.

. . . .

Any type of tomato can be used.

Tomato is a rich source of nutrients and vitamins. The sweet-sour daikon puree pairs well with the full-bodied tomato. A crisp, refreshing dish that is pleasing to the eye as well as palate.

SWEET POTATO and SHUNGIKU with SESAME DRESSING

Serves 4

40 g (1^1/$_2$ oz) *shungiku* (chrysanthemum) leaves

150 g (5^1/$_3$ oz) Japanese sweet potatoes

Vegetable oil for deep frying

SESAME DRESSING

1 tsp sesame paste

1 Tbsp sake

1 tsp mirin

1 tsp Japanese soy sauce

Remove *shungiku* leaves from stems. Wash and drain well.

Boil a pot of water. Parboil *shungiku* stems briefly for about 1 minute, then remove and rinse in cold water. Drain and squeeze out excess water. Chop finely.

Grind *shungiku* stems with a *suribachi* or mortar and pestle. Add sesame paste, sake, mirin and soy sauce and mix well.

Wash and scrub sweet potatoes. Cut into bite-sized pieces.

Heat oil and deep fry sweet potatoes until golden brown. Remove and drain well on absorbent paper.

Gently mix *shungiku* leaves and fried sweet potatoes with the sesame dressing.

Divide into 4 equal portions on individual plates and serve.

. . . .

Substitute *shungiku* with any leafy salad vegetable. You can also parboil the *shungiku* leaves instead of leaving it raw.

Substitute sweet potato with yam or pumpkin.

Crispy sweet potato is paired with raw
shungiku leaves to create a salad-like dish using
sesame dressing. The fresh, herby character of
the *shungiku* leaves cuts through the richness
of the savoury fried sweet potatoes.

CHAWANMUSHI KABOCHA

Serves 4

200 g (7 oz) *kabocha* (Japanese pumpkin)

100 g (3¹/₂ oz) *momen* tofu

32 g (1 oz) edamame

CHAWANMUSHI SAUCE

250 ml (8 fl oz) mushroom dashi (page 16)

1 Tbsp sake

1 tsp Japanese soy sauce

¹/₂ tsp sea salt

2 Tbsp kuzu

Remove excess water from *momen* tofu by wrapping it with paper towels on a shallow bowl. Weigh it down evenly with a plate and refrigerate for at least 30 minutes. Remove from fridge and mash tofu.

Peel and seed *kabocha* and cut into chunky pieces. Steam *kabocha* for about 25 minutes or until tender. Set aside to cool and then mash.

Boil a pot of water. Add edamame and boil for about 5 minutes. Drain and cool under cold running water or immerse in cold water. When cooled, shell edamame by gently squeeze the pods with your fingers. Set aside.

Divide edamame, tofu and *kabocha* equally among 4 individual *chawanmushi* cups. Cover with aluminum foil and steam for about 5 minutes.

Prepare *chawanmushi* sauce. Combine mushroom dashi, salt, soy sauce and sake in a saucepan. Bring it to the boil and then lower heat to a simmer. Mix *kuzu* with water to form a paste. Whisk into the sauce to thicken.

Spoon sauce into the *chawanmushi* cups and serve.

Substitute *kuzu* with *katakuriko* or corn starch.

Other than edamame, you can also add other ingredients such as shiitake mushrooms, gingko nuts, etc.

Chawanmushi is a classic Japanese steamed egg custard
served in a tea cup. Using this method of steaming,
I have substituted the egg with *kabocha* and tofu to
achieve a soft, smooth texture with rich umami.

NASU DENGAKU with ATSUAGE and SHISHITO

Serves 4

3 *nasu* (Japanese eggplant), each about 70 g (2¹/₂ oz)

210 g (7¹/₂ oz) *atsuage*

4 shishito peppers

1 Tbsp sesame oil

DENGAKU MISO DRESSING

1 Tbsp red miso

1 Tbsp sake

1 Tbsp raw sugar

To prepare the *dengaku miso* dressing, mix all the ingredients well and set aside.

Pour boiling water over *atsuage* and cut into eighths.

Cut *nasu* into chunky pieces.

Heat sesame oil in a pan. Add *nasu* and sauté for about 2–3 minutes under medium heat. Then add *atsuage* and continue to sauté for another 2–3 minutes.

Add shishito and stir briefly till it is coated with oil. Lastly, add *dengaku miso* dressing and mix well.

Divide into 4 equal portions on individual plates and serve.

Puncture each shishito before cooking to vent expanding hot air that could cause the pepper to burst. It should be added last as shishito cooks easily.

Substitute shishito with any pepper. However, adding this ingredient is optional.

Dengaku miso (also known as sweetened miso) is a popular dressing used in Japan for vegetable and tofu, made with a stronger flavoured red miso. In this recipe, it is used to glaze sautéed eggplants and fried tofu while shishito peppers are added to lightly spice up the dish.

VINEGARED CUCUMBER and WAKAME

Serves 4

70 g (2¹/₂ oz) Japanese cucumber

5 g (¹/₅ oz) dried wakame seaweed

Sea salt, as needed

VINAIGRETTE

1 Tbsp lemon juice

2 Tbsp rice vinegar

1 tsp mirin

1 Tbsp raw sugar

Thinly slice cucumber. Sprinkle salt and mix well. Let it sit for 10 minutes.

Soak wakame in water for about 10 minutes. Drain and briefly blanch in boiling water. Cut into bite-sized pieces.

To make the dressing, mix lemon juice, vinegar, mirin and sugar until all sugar is dissolved.

Gently squeeze out excess water from cucumber and wakame. Add the dressing and mix well by tossing.

Divide into 4 equal portions on individual plates and serve.

If Japanese cucumber is not available, other varieties of cucumber can be used, but the seeds will have to be removed.

This recipe is good with cucumber alone.

Sunomono refers to vinegared dishes commonly served on the side. This salad recipe uses crunchy Japanese cucumber and nutrient-rich wakame seaweed. A refreshing dish to cool off on a hot summer day.

SIMMERED EGGPLANTS

Serves 4

4 Japanese eggplants, each about 70 g (2½ oz)

SIMMERING STOCK

250 ml (8 fl oz) konbu dashi (page 16)

4 Tbsp Japanese soy sauce

3 Tbsp sake

½ tsp ginger juice (page 17)

1 Tbsp raw sugar

Score each eggplant 3 times; approximately 1–2 cm from the cap to 1–2 cm from its base. The cuts should be equal distant around the eggplant.

In a pot, mix konbu dashi, soy sauce, sake, ginger juice and sugar and bring it to a boil. Lower heat and add eggplants. Simmer for about 15–20 minutes. Turn the eggplants at 5 minutes intervals.

Remove and cut each eggplant in half. Arrange on 4 individual serving plates.

Drizzle 2–3 Tbsp of the simmering broth over eggplants and serve.

Substitute Japanese eggplants with other varieties of aubergine.

Plump and glossy Japanese eggplants look particularly attractive during summer. Though the recipe is relatively simple, it is not so common outside of Japan.
A delight for aubergine lovers!

CORN TOFU with WOLFBERRIES

Serves 4

1 corn on the cob, about
260 g (9 oz)

A pinch of sea salt

10 g (1/3 oz) wolfberries

2 Tbsp mirin

30g (1 oz) *kuzu*

250 ml (8 fl oz) konbu dashi
(page 16)

Wasabi, to taste

SAUCE

2 Tbsp konbu dashi
(page 16)

2 Tbsp Japanese soy sauce

To prepare the sauce, combine konbu dashi and soy sauce in a saucepan. Bring to a boil and then set aside to cool.

Remove the corn husks. Bring a pot of water to the boil and add corn and salt. Lower to medium heat and boil corn for 5–6 minutes or until soft. Remove and let it cool.

Hydrate wolfberries by soaking in mirin and let it sit for 5 minutes. Remove and set aside.

Remove corn kernels and put in a food blender. Add some konbu dashi and puree.

Transfer corn puree to a non-stick saucepan and mix with *kuzu*, wolfberries and the rest of the konbu dashi. Under medium heat, stir continuously with a sturdy wooden spatula for 10–15 minutes until the mixture has thickened and can be scooped up with the spatula. Turn off the heat and continue to stir for another 5 minutes.

Pour the thickened mixture into molds. Cover and refrigerate for about 1 hour or until set.

Remove corn tofu from molds and place on 4 individual shallow bowls. Serve with small amounts of wasabi and soy sauce.

· ·

This recipe is good with corn alone.

A delectable, creamy dish with a tofu-like texture and sweetness lent by the corn. The wolfberries (also known as goji berries) add to the sweetness and deliver some bite to the thickened puree.

Autumn

Pretty falling leaves bring to mind knives
pruning trees, so the season is associated with metal.
The downward drift of cinnamon-hued leaves suggests
we should let go, lighten our burdens and
liberate ourselves for a fresh start.

SAUTÉED SHIMEJI MUSHROOMS

Serves 4

170 g (6 oz) shimeji mushrooms

1 Tbsp Japanese soy sauce

1 Tbsp sake

1 tsp sesame oil

Remove root end of shimeji mushroom cluster and break up the stalks into small sections.

Heat sesame oil in a pan. Add shimeji mushrooms, sake and soy sauce and sauté for about 3–5 minutes.

Divide into 4 equal portions on individual serving plates and serve.

You can substitute shimeji mushrooms with enoki mushrooms.

Do not overcook the mushroom so as to retain its firm bite.

To prepare the root end as a tempura dish, lightly dust away all the dirt. Coat with tempura batter (page 17) and deep fry until light brown.

A quick and simple recipe of sautéing
shimeji mushrooms in sesame oil. The root ends
of the shimeji mushrooms are typically discarded, but
most people will be surprised to know that
it can be prepared as a tempura dish.

MOUNTAIN YAM CROQUETTE

Serves 4

360 g (12½ oz) *nagaimo*

4 reconstituted dried shiitake mushrooms (page 16)

4 Tbsp mushroom dashi (page 16)

1 Tbsp raw sugar

1 Tbsp Japanese soy sauce

1 Tbsp sake

Plain (all-purpose) flour, for dusting

120 g (4⅕ oz) breadcrumbs

Vegetable oil for deep frying

TEMPURA BATTER
(page 17)

Peel nagaimo and roughly chop into chunks. Steam *nagaimo* for about 30–45 minutes.

Finely chop shiitake mushrooms. Heat vegetable oil in a pan. Add mushrooms and stir fry for 2 minutes. Reduce to low heat and add mushroom dashi, soy sauce, sugar and sake. Cook for another 5 minutes until the flavour is absorbed.

Heat a pan over low heat. Mash *nagaimo* in the pan, to remove excess liquid from the *nagaimo*. Turn off heat and add mushrooms. Mix well and refrigerate for at least 2 hours.

Divide the mixture into 8 portions and shape into oblong patties. Dust patties with some flour.

Coat patties with tempura batter, then cover with breadcrumbs.

Heat oil and deep fry patties for about 1–2 minutes or until light brown. Remove and drain well on absorbent paper.

Arrange on 4 individual serving plates and serve.

You can substitute *nagaimo* with other varieties of mountain yam.

If itching occurs when touching *nagaimo*, soothe skin by applying diluted vinegar. Wear gloves for extra protection.

Nagaimo is a healthy root vegetable that aids digestion and nourishes the kidney and spleen. In Japan, it is commonly grated to achieve a gooey texture and eaten raw with wasabi or plain rice. For this recipe, we steam the *nagaimo* and mash it to produce a smooth and creamy paste.

ERINGI MUSHROOMS
with RED MISO

Serves 4

250 g (9 oz) eringi
mushrooms

1¹/₂ Tbsp sesame oil

1 Tbsp lemon juice

MISO DRESSING

30 g (1 oz) carrot, finely
diced

4 fresh shiitake
mushrooms, finely diced

1 Tbsp vegetable oil

1 Tbsp red miso

1 Tbsp raw sugar

2 Tbsp sake

Heat vegetable oil in a pan. Add chopped carrots and
shiitake mushrooms and stir fry for 3 minutes. Reduce
to low heat and add red miso, sugar and sake. Cook for
another 2 minutes. Remove from heat and set aside.

Cut eringi mushrooms into 0.8-cm (¹/₃-in) thick slices.
Heat sesame oil in frying pan and fry eringi mushrooms
for about 5 minutes or until softened.

Drizzle lemon juice over eringi mushrooms and divide
into 4 equal portions. Serve with the miso dressing.

You can use any stocky mushroom as a substitute.

Do not slice the eringi mushroom too thin as they reduce
in size substantially when cooked, losing the desired
"meaty" texture.

It is important to reduce heat before adding the red miso,
so as to preserve its beneficial properties.

Cooked eringi mushroom has an interesting "meaty" texture, similar to that of abalone. It is a toothsome ingredient that is firm to the bite, especially good for meat lovers.

YURINE TEMPURA

Serves 4

2–4 fresh *yurine* (lily bulbs), about 170 g (6 oz)

Vegetable oil for deep frying

Breadcrumbs, as needed

Plain (all-purpose) flour, for dusting

TEMPURA BATTER (page 17)

Wash *yurine* and trim the base. Remove any black spots and steam the *yurine* petals for about 15–20 minutes or until soft. Set aside to cool.

Press steamed *yurine* petals with a spatula through a fine sieve to obtain a smooth paste. Divide the *yurine* paste into 8 portions. Roll each portion into a ball and dust with flour.

Coat the *yurine* balls with tempura batter, then breadcrumbs.

Heat oil and deep fry the balls for about 1–2 minutes or until light brown. Remove and drain well on absorbent paper.

Arrange on 4 individual serving plates and serve.

Sweet potato can be used as a substitute if you are unable to find fresh *yurine*. Mash sweet potato according to instructions above.

See my previous cookbook, *Shojin Ryori: The Art of Japanese Vegetarian Cuisine* for more vegetable tempura ideas.

Edible lily bulbs are typically used in Asian cooking. According to traditional Chinese medicine, it has medicinal benefits for the lungs and heart. But far from bitter-tasting Chinese medicine, these tempura balls are crispy on the outside, creamy on the inside and delicately sweet.

BRAISED SATOIMO and ATSUAGE

Serves 4

6 *satoimo* (baby taro roots), about 280 g (10 oz)

210 g (7¹/₂ oz) *atsuage*

10 g (¹/₃ oz) grated ginger

200 ml (6²/₃ fl oz) konbu dashi (page 16)

1 Tbsp sake

1 Tbsp mirin

2 Tbsp soy sauce

Pour boiling water over *atsuage* and cut into eighths.

Wash the *satoimo* and boil it in a pan for about 7 minutes. Remove from heat and place the *satoimo* in cold water. Peel the skin and cut into bite-sized pieces.

Boil konbu dashi in a pot and add *satoimo*. Reduce heat and simmer for about 10 minutes or until soft.

Add *atsuage*, grated ginger, sake, mirin and soy sauce (to taste) and continue to simmer for another 10–15 minutes.

Arrange *satoimo* and *atsuage* in 4 individual shallow bowls and serve with some broth.

Be careful not to break the *satoimo*. To see if it is cooked through, test with a skewer, which should pierce through a piece smoothly without breaking it.

The grated ginger can be served separately.

Satoimo (taro roots) is high in fibre and potassium, both of which help to lower the risk of hypertension. Some people may experience itchy skin when touching *satoimo*. Boiling it briefly before peeling prevents this irritation. When cooked, *satoimo* has a smooth, creamy texture that breaks easily in the mouth.

STUFFED PEPPERS with YAMATOIMO

Serves 4

8 green peppers

600 g (1¹⁄₃ pounds) *yamatoimo*

Vegetable oil for deep frying

SIMMERING BROTH

50 ml (1²⁄₃ fl oz) konbu dashi (page 16)

50 ml (1²⁄₃ fl oz) Japanese soy sauce

1 Tbsp mirin

1 Tbsp raw sugar

Cut the top stem section and trim off tail end of the peppers. Gently remove pith and seeds.

Peel and grate *yamatoimo*. Place grated *yamatoimo* in a resealable bag and cut off one corner tip. Gently squeeze *yamatoimo* to fill the pepper.

Heat oil and deep fry stuffed peppers for about 30 seconds or when outer skins are a little charred. Remove and drain on absorbent paper.

Prepare konbu dashi and add soy sauce, mirin and sugar. Bring to the boil and add the fried peppers. Lower heat and simmer for 5 minutes.

Arrange 2 pieces of peppers each in 4 individual shallow bowls. Drizzle with some simmering broth and serve.

Use any type of chilli pepper that is not too spicy.

When stuffing the green peppers with *yamatoimo*, gently tap the pepper so that it is evenly filled.

Stuffed peppers is a dish that can be found in many cuisines around the world. Here, I substitute the meat that is often used, with *yamatoimo*, which has a springy texture when grated and deep fried.

NAGAIMO and OKRA with UMEZUKE

Serves 4

200 g (7 oz) *nagaimo*

4 okra (ladies' fingers),
about 255 g (9 oz)

A handful of shredded
seaweed

PLUM DRESSING

1 *umezuke* (pickled plum)

1 Tbsp sake

1 Tbsp raw sugar

Remove the pit from *umezuke* and crush the flesh,
then add sake and sugar and mix well. Set aside.

Wash and trim stem ends of okra.

Boil a pot of water and add salt. Add okra and blanch
it for about 2 minutes. Remove and set aside to cool.
Then cut into thin slices.

Peel *nagaimo* and remove any black spots. Cut into
thick sticks of about 5 cm (2 in) long.

Mix *nagaimo* and okra with *umezuke* dressing.
Toss gently.

Serve on 4 individual plates and garnish with shredded
nori seaweed strips if desired.

· ·

If using nori seaweed as garnish, sprinkle on only just before
serving to prevent unappealing sogginess and sticking.

Substituting *nagaimo* with other types of yam may require
the yam to be cooked first.

The skin of the *nagaimo* can be cleaned, deep fried and
served as a side dish.

If itching occurs when touching *nagaimo,* soothe skin by
applying diluted vinegar. Wear gloves for extra protection.

Nagaimo, a type of yam which is popular in China and Japan, can be eaten raw and has a crunchy texture. Here is a healthy and nutritious dish that uses *umezuke* (pickled plum) to give a delicate sourness and flavour to otherwise bland *nagaimo* and okra.

SHISO MAKI

Serves 4

8 shiso leaves

320 g (11^1/$_3$ oz) *momen* tofu

1 medium eringi mushroom, finely chopped (about 50 g / 1^3/$_4$ oz)

10-cm (4-in) length burdock

10 g (^{1}/$_3$ oz) grated ginger

2 pieces *kuruma fu*

2 Tbsp cornflour

5 Tbsp soymilk (unsweetened)

^{1}/$_2$ tsp sea salt

1 Tbsp Japanese soy sauce

Vegetable oil for sautéing

4 lemon wedges

SIMMERING STOCK

250 ml (8 fl oz) konbu dashi (page 16)

1 tsp Japanese soy sauce

1 Tbsp sake

SAUCE

1 Tbsp Japanese soy sauce

1 Tbsp miri

Remove excess water from *momen* tofu by wrapping it with paper towels on a shallow bowl. Weight it down evenly with a plate and refrigerate for at least 30 minutes.

Peel burdock and soak in water immediately to prevent discolouration. Discard water and drain well before using.

Prepare konbu dashi. Add soy sauce and sake. Bring to the boil and add burdock. Lower heat and simmer for 20 minutes. Remove burdock and finely chop when it is cooled.

Using a food processor, grind the *kuruma fu* into crumbs.

Remove tofu from the refrigerator and peel off the paper towels. Mash tofu and add burdock, eringi mushroom, grated ginger, *kuruma fu* crumbs, cornflour, soymilk, sea salt and soy sauce. Mix well and refrigerate for 30 minutes.

Divide mixture into 8 portions and shape into balls. Place one ball on each shiso leaf and flatten into patties.

Heat vegetable oil in a pan. Sauté shiso patties on medium heat for 3–4 minutes on each side. Mix soy sauce and mirin. Drizzle the sauce on the shiso patties and sauté briefly.

Arrange on 4 individual serving plates with a wedge of lemon each and serve.

. . . .

Alternative method for making *kuruma fu* crumbs is to place *kuruma fu* in a plastic bag and smash.

You can substitute *kuruma fu* with bread crumbs.

If the shiso patty mixture is too dry, add more soymilk.

The flavour of this tasty dish is enhanced by the distinctive fragrance of shiso leaf (also known as perilla). The use of burdock and eringi mushroom adds a nice depth to its taste and texture. A healthy alternative to burger patties!

Winter

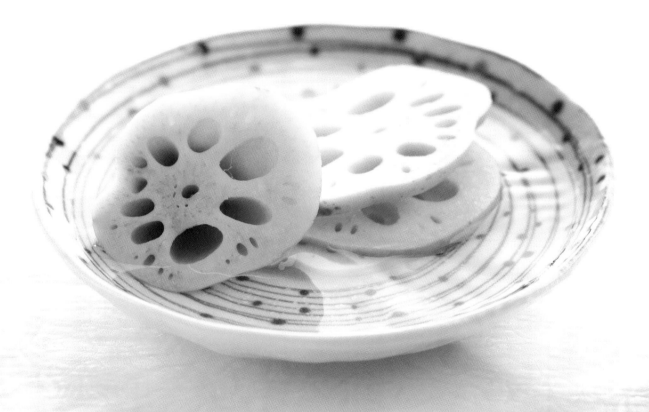

Winter is associated with the element of water, and all is calm and serene. The season seems to wrap us up in a blanket of tranquility, reminding us to slow down and enjoy the refreshing stillness, while plants and animals hibernate and prepare for a new spring.

DAIKON with RED MISO

Serves 4

12-cm (5-in) length daikon

1 tsp rice

MISO DRESSING

2 Tbsp red miso

1 Tbsp raw sugar

2 Tbsp sake

Peel and slice daikon to 4 equal rounds. Cut each daikon round into quarters without cutting all the way through. Use a red string to go around the daikon over the cross sections that you have cut. Secure the string with a knot at the centre.

Boil a pot of water and add daikon and rice. Simmer for about 20 minutes or until daikon is tender.

To prepare the miso dressing, mix all the ingredients in a saucepan over low heat. Stir gently until all sugar is dissolved. Turn off the heat.

Arrange daikon rounds on 4 individual plates and serve with the miso dressing.

To eat, hold the daikon round with a chopstick at its centre and pull the red string. The daikon round will break neatly into 4 quarters.

Instead of adding rice to the boiling water, ricewater left over from washing rice can be used.

The amount of water used should be just enough for the daikon to be totally submerged without floating around too much. Otherwise, it may break the daikon.

You may see them all year round but winter is the best season for sweet and juicy daikon. Using string to cut the daikon into quarters will intrigue guests, injecting a delightful surprise to this Japanese comfort dish.

DAIKON IN MISO BROTH

Serves 4

10-cm (4-in) length daikon
(about 325g / 11¹/₂ oz)

3-cm (1¹/₅-in) slice red chilli

1 tsp sesame oil

MISO BROTH

200 ml (6²/₃ fl oz)
konbu dashi

1 Tbsp white miso

1 Tbsp mirin

1 Tbsp sake

1 tsp potato starch

Peel and cut daikon into bite-sized pieces.

Slice chilli lengthwise into half and remove the seeds. Heat sesame oil in a pot. Add chilli and stir fry for 30 seconds. Remove chilli and then add daikon pieces. Cook until the daikon is a little charred around edges.

Pour konbu dashi and bring to the boil. Reduce heat and simmer for 15–20 minutes or until tender.

Pass miso through a fine sieve into the broth and stir until dissolved. Add mirin and sake and mix well.

Mix potato starch with a little water and add to the broth, whisking until thickened.

Divide into 4 equal portions in individual shallow bowls and serve with the miso broth spooned over.

If the miso broth is too watery, you can simmer longer to thicken it.

You can choose to omit the chilli if you wish.

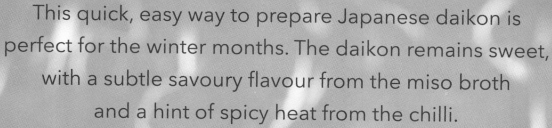

This quick, easy way to prepare Japanese daikon is perfect for the winter months. The daikon remains sweet, with a subtle savoury flavour from the miso broth and a hint of spicy heat from the chilli.

LOTUS ROOT with YAMATOIMO

Serves 4

7-cm (2³/₄-in) length lotus root

150 g (5¹/₃ oz) *yamatoimo*

Vegetable oil for deep frying

GINGER SAUCE

1 Tbsp ginger juice

2 Tbsp Japanese soy sauce

To prepare sauce, mix ginger juice and soy sauce and set aside.

Peel *yamatoimo* and finely grate.

Wash and peel lotus root. Slice into 0.3-cm thick slices. Spread 1 Tbsp of grated *yamatoimo* on a lotus root slice and place another slice on it, like a sandwich, pressing lightly.

Heat vegetable oil and slide the lotus root with *yamatoimo* into the hot oil. Deep fry for 1–2 minutes until light brown. Remove and drain on absorbent paper.

Arrange on 4 individual serving plates. Drizzle ginger sauce over and serve.

The grated *yamatoimo* will hold the two lotus root slices together quite well. Do not press too hard.

The subtle characters of lotus root with *yamatoimo* pair very well with the ginger sauce. This simple yet delicate dish is sure to charm and impress.

KUROMAME
(Sweet Black Soybean)

Serves 4

100 g (3$\frac{1}{2}$ oz) *kuromame* (black soybean)

80 g (2$\frac{4}{5}$ oz) raw sugar

1 Tbsp Japanese soy sauce

$\frac{1}{4}$ tsp sea salt

Rinse *kuromame* and discard any spoilt ones. Then soak it in ample water for at least 3 hours or overnight. Discard the water.

Boil *kuromame* with ample water in a pot and add sugar, soy sauce and salt. Bring to a boil and then reduce heat. Simmer under low heat for about 3 hours or until soft. Remove any white foam that appears during simmering.

Remove from heat and let it cool. Refrigerate overnight so that the beans will absorb more flavour.

Soaking the beans reduces the simmering time required. The simmering time may vary depending on how long the beans have been soaked.

A traditional method is to add some rusty nails (wrapped in cloth) into the boiling water, to give the beans a dark, glossy sheen. However, I find that the *kuromame* is shiny enough without the use of rusty nails.

Kuromame has an attractive, shiny appearance and is often served in *osechi ryori* (traditional new year cuisine). "Mame" means health, so serving *Kuromame* symbolises good health. The beans are high in fibre and said to have many health benefits.

BURDOCK ROOT TERIYAKI

Serves 4

35-cm (14-in) burdock root (*gobo*)

1 tsp vegetable oil

1 Tbsp Japanese soy sauce

1 Tbsp mirin

1 tsp raw sugar

Peel burdock root and make 2–3 cuts lengthwise (about 4-5 cm from one end). Shave burdock root with a knife (like sharpening a pencil) or with a vegetable peeler. Soak the shavings in water immediately for 10 minutes to prevent discolouration. Discard water and drain well.

Heat vegetable oil in a pan. Add burdock root and stir fry for 3 minutes. Add soy sauce and mirin and continue to stir fry for 2 minutes, until the burdock root's texture is crispy. Lastly, reduce heat and add sugar. Stir fry for another 1 minute or until the sugar is completely dissolved.

Divide into 4 equal portions and serve.

Vary the amount of sugar to taste.

Do ensure that the stir-fried burdock root shavings achieve a crispy texture before adding the sugar.

Burdock root (known in Japanese as *gobo*) is an amazing health food that boosts immunity. This simple yet nourishing dish of thinly shredded burdock root is easy and full-flavoured, going very well with even just plain rice.

GOBO with UMEZUKE

Serves 4

25-cm (10-in) length burdock root (*gobo*)

2 *umezuke* (pickled plum)

2 Tbsp sake

1 Tbsp vegetable oil

150 ml (5 fl oz) konbu dashi

Peel burdock root and cut into thick sticks of about 4 cm long. Soak in water immediately to prevent discolouration. Discard water and drain well before using.

Remove the pit from *umezuke* and crush the flesh to make a paste. Set aside.

Heat vegetable oil in a pan. Sauté burdock root for 5 minutes.

Add konbu dashi, sake and *umezuke* paste. Simmer for 10–20 minutes or until the liquid is gone.

Arrange on 4 individual serving plates and serve.

You can substitute whole *umezuke* with *umezuke* puree or any type of plum puree found in supermarkets.

This is another simple way to prepare burdock root (*gobo*), which is known to detoxify blood, the lymphatic system and skin. Its earthy, herby flavour works well with delicate, sour *umezuke* (pickled plum) which aids digestion and combats fatigue.
A superfood dish that goes well with just plain rice.

KARASHI RENKON

Serves 4

7-9 cm (2³/₄-3¹/₂-in) length (about 200 g / 7 oz) lotus root, washed and peeled

Plain (all purpose) flour, for dusting

Vegetable oil for deep frying

SIMMERING STOCK

400 ml (13¹/₂ fl oz) konbu dashi

2 Tbsp rice vinegar

3 Tbsp raw sugar

1 tsp sea salt

MUSTARD MISO STUFFING

3 g (¹/₁₀ oz) *karashi* powder

1 tsp warm water (to mix with *karashi* powder)

2 Tbsp sweet miso

50 g (1³/₄ oz) *momen* tofu

TEMPURA BATTER
(page 17)

Remove excess water from *momen* tofu by wrapping it with paper towels. Place it in a shallow bowl. Weigh it down evenly with a plate. After 30 minutes, peel off the paper towels and mash tofu.

Prepare konbu dashi. Add vinegar, sugar and salt and bring to the boil. Then add lotus root, lower heat and simmer for 20 minutes. Remove and set aside to cool.

To prepare the mustard miso stuffing, mix *karashi* powder with warm water well. Add miso and *momen* tofu and mix them well to form a mound.

Press the lotus root onto the mound such that the stuffing is forced to fill up the holes of the lotus root. Repeat this action until the stuffing is pushed to the top. Scrape off the excess stuffing at the top and refrigerate for at least 2 hours or overnight.

Remove any excess stuffing and dust the lotus root with flour. Hold the lotus root with 2 skewers inserted at its side (to coat with tempura batter and hold in oil while deep frying). Coat the lotus root with the tempura batter.

Heat oil and deep fry coated lotus root for about 1 minute or until light brown. Remove and drain on absorbent paper.

Cut lotus root into 8 slices. Arrange equal portions on 4 individual serving plates. Serve.

Substitute *karashi* powder with any mustard available or with wasabi. Substitute sweet miso with any miso available but add sugar and mirin. Hold the coated lotus root with skewers in deep frying oil without first touching the bottom of the pot. Once all surfaces are cooked, the lotus root can be released from the skewers.

Karashi renkon is lotus root stuffed with mustard miso. This nutritious dish was said to be first created by a Zen monk for a Japanese lord who had a poor appetite. It needs a bit more preparation work but the actual cooking time is rather short. Enjoy the process!

SAUTÉED CABBAGE

Serves 4

200 g (7 oz) cabbage
leaves

50 g (1³/₄ oz) carrot

4 pieces reconstituted
dried mushrooms

20 g (²/₃ oz) *abura-age*

1 tsp sesame oil

1 Tbsp sake

1 Tbsp Japanese soy sauce

PLUM PASTE

1 *umezuke* (pickled plum)

1 Tbsp sake

Remove the pit from the *umezuke* and crush the flesh, then add sake and mix well. Set aside.

Julienne *abura-age*, carrot and mushrooms.

Cut cabbage leaves into halves lengthwise (along the stem) and then cut crosswise into thin slices, about 1–2 cm (¹/₂ – ³/₄ in) widths.

Heat sesame oil in a pan. Add *abura-age*, carrot and mushrooms and stir fry for 2 minutes. Add cabbage, sake and soy sauce and sauté for another 5 minutes or until tender.

Reduce heat and add *umezuke* paste. Mix well.

Divide into 4 equal portions on individual serving plates and serve.

If the cabbage is too dry during sautéing, add water or more sake.

Soy sauce can be adjusted to taste.

The cabbage leaves give out a sweet flavour from being sautéed while the sour *umezuke* (pickled plum) is a fine complement to it. This is a versatile and flavourful dish that works well with other dishes in a *shojin ryori* set.

All Seasons

Infuse mindfulness and gratitude into
daily life with recipes that can be prepared all year
round, or paired flexibly with other dishes and
ingredients at their seasonal best.
Enjoy the present moment and the gifts it brings,
and soak in daily, simple pleasures.

GOMA DOFU (Sesame Tofu)

Serves 4

30 g (1 oz) *kuzu*

2 Tbsp black sesame paste

250 ml (8 fl oz) water

Ice cubes, as needed

Yuzu kosho, to taste

SAUCE

3 Tbsp konbu dashi

3 Tbsp Japanese soy sauce

To make the sauce, combine konbu dashi and soy sauce in a saucepan. Bring to a boil and then set aside to cool.

Mix *kuzu*, sesame paste and water together in a non-stick saucepan, stirring until the mixture is smooth. Place sesame mixture over medium heat. Stir vigorously and continuously with a sturdy wooden spatula for 10–15 minutes until the mixture is thick. It should coat the spatula and not drip off rapidly when you scoop it up. Turn off the heat and continue to stir for another 2 minutes. Divide into 4 equal portions.

Place a sheet of plastic wrap over a small porcelain bowl. Gently make an indentation in the centre so that you can pour each sesame mixture portion into the bowl. Twist the wrap to shape each portion into a firm ball. Secure it with a flexible wire and place it in a container of water filled with ice cubes so as to force-cool the *goma dofu*. Set aside for about 3 hours.

Unwrap each ball. Serve with the sauce and *yuzu kosho*.

Substitute *yuzu kosho* with condiments like wasabi or mustard.

Do not put the *goma dofu* in the refrigerator to cool as it will harden and not have the desired springy texture.

Goma dofu is also commonly made with white sesame paste, as pictured on this book's cover and in my previous cookbook, *Shojin Ryori: The Art of Japanese Vegetarian Cuisine*.

Goma dofu has a springy, tofu-like texture, yet is made without soybeans. It epitomises the spirit of *shojin ryori* as it uses minimal ingredients for maximum flavour. Here, I have used black sesame paste and citrusy *yuzu kosho*. The round, pretty shape is adaptable to odd numbers of guests.

SAUTÉED SHIITAKE MUSHROOMS

Serves 4

12 pieces reconstituted dried shiitake mushroom (page 16)

1 tsp vegetable oil

1¹/₂ Tbsp sake

1 Tbsp soy sauce

Heat vegetable oil in a pan. Add mushrooms and stir fry both sides for 2 minutes. Then add sake and soy sauce and continue to fry for another 30 seconds.

Divide into 4 equal portions and serve.

Add sake first for the stir fry as it will help to soften the mushrooms.

This simple, effortless dish is a delicious accompaniment to other *shojin* dishes or even plain rice. Guests are usually amazed when they learn how easy this recipe is.

MISO MARINATED TOFU

Serves 4

1 block *momen* tofu

MISO MIXTURE

Red miso, as required

For every 50 g (1³⁄₄ oz) miso:

1 Tbsp sake

1 tsp raw sugar

Remove excess water from *momen* tofu by wrapping it with paper towels and placing it in a shallow bowl. Weigh it down evenly with a plate and refrigerate for at least 30 minutes.

Prepare the miso mixture in a saucepan and place it over very low heat to dissolve the sugar. Set aside to cool.

Remove tofu from the refrigerator and peel off the paper towels. Cover tofu with miso completely in a plastic wrap and let it sit for at least half a day, or overnight.

Remove miso from the tofu and wipe away any residue with kitchen paper towel. Cut into 0.5-cm thick slices, divide into 4 equal portions and serve. Garnish with a dab of *yuzu kosho* if desired.

Any type of miso can be used, but if a strong-flavoured type of miso is used, you can serve the tofu in smaller pieces.

This tofu dish shows off the miso flavour beautifully and subtly. Feel free to use your favourite type of miso. For convenience, prepare this dish beforehand to let the tofu sit and absorb the flavours.

SHOJIN STEAK

Serves 4

2 pieces *kuruma fu*

Plain (all-purpose) flour, as needed

1 Tbsp vegetable oil

SEASONING MIXTURE

100 ml (3^1/$_3$ fl oz) konbu dashi

50 ml (1^3/$_4$ fl oz) soy sauce

Soak *kuruma fu* in water for about 15 minutes or until soft. Cut each ring into quarters and squeeze to remove as much excess liquid as possible.

To prepare the seasoning mixture, combine konbu dashi and soy sauce in a saucepan. Bring to a boil and then set aside to cool.

Soak *kuruma fu* quarters in the seasoning mixture for about 15 minutes. Gently squeeze to remove liquid partially and then coat with flour on both sides.

Heat vegetable oil in a frying pan and sauté *kuruma fu* quarters on both sides for a total of 1 minute. Divide into 4 equal portions and serve.

When sautéing *kuruma fu* quarters, clean the frying pan between batches.

Serve hot while the *kuruma fu* quarters are still crisp.

Due to its close resemblance to braised meat, *shojin* steak is like mock meat for *shojin* cooking. This dish never fails to delight and surprise. Have some fun making your guests believe you are serving them a non-vegetarian dish.

AGEDASHI TOFU

Serves 4

1 block silken tofu

Vegetable oil for deep frying

Katakuriko for coating

SAUCE

100 ml (3$^{1}/_{3}$ fl oz) mushroom dashi (page 16)

2 Tbsp mirin

2 Tbsp Japanese soy sauce

TOPPING

Shredded nori seaweed

Grated ginger pulp (using 20 g / $^{2}/_{3}$ oz ginger)

Grated daikon pulp (using 60 g / 2 oz daikon and applying the same method as grated ginger on page 17)

To prepare the sauce, mix mushroom dashi, soy sauce and mirin in a pot and bring to a boil. Set aside.

Cut the tofu into 8 blocks and coat all sides with *katakuriko*.

Heat oil for deep frying. Add tofu pieces and fry for about 2 minutes or until golden brown. Drain the excess oil with paper towels on a plate.

Arrange equal pieces of tofu in 4 individual shallow bowls. Drizzle sauce over each serving and garnish with shredded nori seaweed, grated daikon and ginger.

You can heat up the sauce and add to the tofu pieces just before serving.

Substitute *katakuriko* with cornflour. However, using *katakuriko* would produce the best result.

Agedashi tofu is deep fried tofu served in a savoury dashi broth. It is a very simple yet popular dish in Japanese cuisine.

KOYADOFU TEMPURA

Serves 4

2 pieces dried *koyadofu*

Vegetable oil for deep frying

SIMMERING STOCK

200 ml (6²/₃ fl oz) konbu dashi

1 Tbsp Japanese soy sauce

1 tsp mirin

1 tsp sake

TEMPURA BATTER (page 17)

4 shiso leaves

Soak *koyadofu* in warm water for 15 minutes or until soft. Rinse in clean water and gently squeeze out water. Repeat this process 2 or 3 times. Then press out water and cut each *koyadofu* into 4 blocks.

Prepare konbu dashi in a saucepan. Add soy sauce, mirin and sake and bring to a boil. Reduce heat and add *koyadofu* pieces. Simmer for 10 minutes. Remove and set aside to cool.

Finely chop shiso leaves. Add chopped shiso to tempura batter and mix well.

Gently press out half the liquid from the simmered *koyadofu*. Coat the koyadofu pieces with tempura batter.

Heat oil and deep fry coated *koyadofu* until light brown. Remove and drain on absorbent paper.

Arrange on 4 individual serving plates. Best eaten while the pieces are hot.

You can substitute shiso leaves with other green herbs such as mint or parsley.

Koyadofu is dried frozen tofu which was discovered when tofu was found frozen under extreme cold on Mount Koya. When reconstituted with water, it has a spongy texture that absorbs flavour beautifully. It is a highly nutritious ingredient commonly used in Japanese cooking. This simple yet elegant dish has a crispy coating accented with shiso leaves and a spongy interior.

INARI-ZUSHI

Serves 4

4 *abura-age* (7 cm / 2³/₄ in by 4 cm / 1¹/₂ in)

150 g (5¹/₃ oz) Japanese short-grain rice

3-cm (1¹/₄-in) piece of konbu

160 ml (5¹/₂ fl oz) water

3 Tbsp toasted and ground sesame seeds

SIMMERING STOCK

200 ml (6²/₃ fl oz) mushroom dashi (page 16)

2 Tbsp Japanese soy sauce

2 Tbsp mirin

2 Tbsp raw sugar

Prepare Japanese rice by washing and draining in a sieve for 15 minutes. Add konbu and water to rice and soak for 30 minutes. Pour konbu, water and rice into rice cooker and cook according to manufacturer's directions.

When rice is done, fluff up and add toasted and ground sesame seeds. Mix well. Set aside to let it cool to room temperature.

Flatten each piece of *abura-age* with a rolling pin and cut into halves to get 8 halves. Gently open each *abura-age* to form a pouch. Pour boiling water onto *abura-age* to remove excess oil. Drain well.

Prepare mushroom dashi in a saucepan. Add soy sauce, mirin and sugar and bring to a boil. Reduce heat and add *abura-age* pieces. Simmer for 15 minutes. Remove and set aside to cool for at least 3 hours. Before use, gently squeeze out excess liquid (the *abura-age* pouches should still be moist).

Fill up the *abura-age* pouches with rice. Wrap up the opening by overlapping the ends and serve 2 pouches per portion.

You can prepare the *abura-age* pouches in advance and refrigerate overnight.

Do not over boil the *abura-age* pouches as they may break.

You can also add vegetables such as carrot, mushroom, *hijiki* or burdock root to the rice.

In Japanese, *inari* means rice load. *Inari* is the Shinto god of harvest, fertility, rice, agriculture and worldly success. Shinto temples house fox statues believed to be messengers for wishes. *Inari-zushi*, shaped like mice, are made as offerings to these fox messengers. Others believe *inari-zushi* look like fox's ears, symbolising bags of good news.

KONNYAKU with MISO SAUCE

Serves 4

250 g (9 oz) *konnyaku*

MISO SAUCE

1 tsp sesame oil

2 Tbsp red miso

2 Tbsp sake

1 Tbsp raw sugar

1 tsp lemon juice

Prepare the miso sauce by heating sesame oil in a saucepan. Lower heat and add red miso, sake and sugar. Stir to mix well until sugar is dissolved and set aside. When it is cooled, add lemon juice and mix well.

Rinse *konnyaku* and knead firmly. Cut into 1-cm (1/2-in) thick slices.

Boil a pot of water and add in *konnyaku* pieces. Simmer for about 5 minutes. Remove and pat dry with a towel.

Arrange on 4 individual serving plates and serve with the miso sauce spooned over.

Instead of boiling the *konnyaku*, you can also dry roast it in a pan on the stove without using any oil.

Konnyaku is a jellied yam cake that may come in
different colours depending on the added ingredients.
It has little taste on its own, but is commonly used
in Japanese cooking for its springy texture.
High in dietary fibre with almost zero calories,
it is a popular choice among weight watchers.

Soups

In a traditional Japanese meal, rice and soup are always served. In the past, the left side of the tray was reserved for the more important items. The Japanese have regarded rice as an important staple for generations, and so the rice is always placed on the left side with the soup on the right. With my guests, I normally recommend starting with some soup. This helps warm up the stomach before proceeding with the rest of the meal.

SPICY MISO SOUP

Serves 4

1.25 litres (40 fl oz) mushroom dashi (page 16)

2 medium dried shiitake mushrooms

100 g (3 1/2 oz) daikon

80 g (2 4/5 oz) carrot

5-cm (2-in) length lotus root

1 Japanese eggplant

4 Tbsp white miso

3-cm (1 1/2-in) slice red chilli

1 Tbsp sesame oil

Prepare mushroom dashi. Reserve 2 mushrooms and cut into quarters. Set aside.

Peel carrot, daikon and lotus root. Cut each root vegetable into bite-sized pieces. Cut the eggplant into 1-cm thick slices.

Slice chilli lengthwise into half and remove the seeds. Heat sesame oil in a pot. Add chilli and stir fry for 30 seconds. Remove chilli and then add the rest of the vegetables (carrot, daikon, lotus root and eggplant). Cook for another 2-3 minutes.

Add mushroom dashi and bring to a boil. Lower heat and simmer for 15-20 minutes, skimming off and discarding any foam that surfaces from time to time.

Press white miso through a fine sieve into the stock and stir until dissolved.

Spoon soup and vegetables into 4 serving bowls and serve.

. . . .

Once the miso has been added, do not boil the soup as it will destroy the beneficial properties of the miso. Substitute or add any other vegetable that you like.

CARROT SOUP

Serves 4

100 g (3¹/₂ oz) carrot

400 ml (13¹/₂ fl oz) soymilk (unsweetened)

400 ml (13¹/₂ fl oz) konbu dashi

Sea salt, as needed

Peel and cut carrot into chunks. Boil a pot of water and add in carrot. Simmer for about 15 minutes or until the carrot is soft. Remove carrot and leave to cool.

Add carrot and soymilk in a food processor. Blend until smooth. Transfer to a pot and add konbu dashi. Simmer for 10 minutes under medium heat and stir gently. Add salt to taste.

Spoon soup into 4 serving bowls and serve.

. . . .

Avoid over boiling as it might burn the soymilk. Low medium heat will be sufficient.

Sautéed mushrooms can also be added. Julienne 2 fresh shiitake mushrooms and stir fry with sesame oil for a minute before adding sake and soy sauce. Cook for a further 30 seconds, then spoon into carrot soup.

DAIKON SOUP

Serves 4

500 ml (16 fl oz) konbu dashi

600 g (1¹/₃ pound) daikon

2 g (¹/₁₀ oz) ginger

1 tsp sesame oil

Sea salt, as needed

Prepare konbu dashi and set aside.

Peel and cut daikon into chunks. Boil a pot of water and add in daikon. Simmer for about 20 minutes or until the daikon is soft. Remove daikon and leave to cool. Once cool, puree daikon in a food processor until smooth.

Peel and cut ginger into thin slices. Heat sesame oil in a pot and stir fry ginger for about 30 seconds. Transfer konbu dashi and daikon puree into the pot. Bring it to a boil and simmer for 5 minutes under low heat while stirring.

Add salt to taste, spoon into 4 serving bowls and serve hot.

. . . .

If heat is too high, daikon soup can get burned easily. Gently stir while simmering under low heat.

CLEAR APPLE SOUP

Serves 4

1.25 litres (40 fl oz) konbu dashi

100 g (3¹/₂ oz) daikon

Half an apple

80 g (2⁴/₅ oz) carrot

2 Tbsp Japanese soy sauce

1 Tbsp mirin

1 Tbsp sake

Sea salt, as needed

Prepare konbu dashi and set aside.

Peel apple, daikon and carrot and cut each of them into 8 pieces.

In a pot, add apple, daikon, carrot, soy sauce, mirin and sake into konbu dashi and bring to a boil. Lower heat and simmer for 20 minutes. Skim off and discard any foam that surfaces from time to time.

Add salt to taste, spoon into 4 serving bowls and serve hot.

. . . .

The sweetness of apple adds an interesting depth to this soup. You can substitute daikon and carrot with other root vegetables.

BARLEY MISO SOUP

Serves 4

65 g (2¹⁄₃ oz) barley

250 ml (8 fl oz) water, for boiling barley

4 Tbsp white miso

1 litre (32 fl oz) water

SAUTÉED MUSHROOMS

2 fresh shiitake mushrooms

1 tsp oil

1 tsp sake

1 tsp soy sauce

Rinse barley well and soak it. Place 250 ml (8 fl oz) water and barley in a medium saucepan and bring to a boil. Reduce to medium heat and simmer for 30-40 minutes or until the barley is tender.

Chop mushrooms. Heat oil in a pot and stir fry mushroom for about 1 minute. Add sake and soy sauce and cook for another 30 seconds.

Add 1 litre (32 fl oz) of water to the mushrooms and bring to a boil. Reduce heat and add barley. Simmer for another 10 minutes.

Press white miso through a fine sieve into the pot and stir until dissolved.

Spoon soup into 4 serving bowls and serve.

. . . .

Either pearl or hulled barley can be used. Check packaging for cooking time.

Pickles

In my early days learning *shojin* cooking, I had a meal with a few others in a Zen temple. A Japanese lady sneaked up to me and whispered in my ear, urging me not to touch the pickle in my *shojin* set. She quietly went back to her seat without giving me a chance to ask further questions. At the end of the meal, a monk came into the room with a pot of tea and started pouring tea into one of the bowls in each person's set. We were supposed to pick up a slice of pickle with chopsticks and give a gentle stir to get any leftover food bits in the bowl. Transfer the tea to another bowl and repeat this action of cleaning the bowl with the pickle and tea until the last bowl, from which we would finish the tea and leftover food.

This ceremony simply emphasises the *shojin* philosophy of minimising wastage which, in my opinion, is so beautiful. While it is not a must to include pickles as part of the meal, this accompaniment lends an elegant touch to it.

PICKLED DAIKON

500 g (1¹/₁₀ pounds) daikon

Yuzu peel, one piece

VINEGAR MIXTURE

2 Tbsp rice vinegar

1 tsp sake

1 tsp sea salt

6 Tbsp raw sugar

Combine ingredients for the vinegar mixture and simmer over low heat to dissolve sugar and salt. Set aside to cool.

Peel and cut daikon into bite-size wedges (about 0.5–1 cm thick).

Put daikon, *yuzu* and vinegar mixture in a resealable bag. Remove any air from the bag, seal and refrigerate for 1–2 days.

. . . .

Lemon peel can be used as a substitute for *yuzu*.

MARINATED CUCUMBER

1 Japanese cucumber, about 90 g (3¹/₄ oz)

Sea salt, as needed

White miso, as needed

Wash and knead cucumber briefly with a small amount of sea salt.

Cover cucumber with miso completely in a resealable bag. Remove any air from the bag, seal and refrigerate for 1–2 days.

Before serving, remove miso from the cucumber and wipe away any residue with kitchen paper towels. Cut into 0.5-cm (¹/₄-in) thick slices.

. . . .

Red miso can also be used to marinate the cucumber.

PICKLED BURDOCK

40-cm (16-in) burdock root

1 Tsp rice vinegar

VINEGAR MIXTURE

4 Tbsp rice vinegar

2 Tbsp raw sugar

1 tsp sea salt

1 tsp Japanese soy sauce

2 Tbsp lemon juice

2 slices young ginger

Combine all ingredients for the vinegar mixture, except lemon juice and ginger, in a saucepan. Place over low heat to dissolve all the sugar and salt. Set aside to cool.

Peel burdock root and cut into sticks of about 3–5 cm long. Soak in water immediately to prevent discolouration. Drain and discard water.

Boil a pot of water and add vinegar. Add burdock root sticks and boil for 5 minutes.

Remove burdock root sticks and put together with the vinegar mixture, lemon juice and ginger slices in a resealable bag. Remove any air from the bag, seal and refrigerate for at least 1–2 hours.

. . . .

Aside from using ginger, you can also marinate burdock root with other aromatic herbs.

HANARENKON
(Flower-Shaped Lotus Root)

90 g (3¼ oz) lotus root

2 Tbsp rice vinegar

VINEGAR MIXTURE

4 Tbsp rice vinegar

2 Tbsp water

2 Tbsp raw sugar

2 Tbsp lemon juice

Sea salt, as needed

Combine all ingredients for the vinegar mixture, except lemon juice, in a saucepan. Place it over low heat to dissolve all the sugar and salt. Set aside to cool.

Peel and slice lotus root into 0.5 cm thick rings. Soak immediately in water (add 1 Tbsp vinegar) to prevent discolouration. Make flower cuts and drain before using.

Boil a pot of water and add the other Tbsp of vinegar. Add sliced lotus root flowers and boil for 5 minutes. Remove lotus root and leave to cool.

Put lotus root slices, vinegar mixture and lemon juice in a resealable bag. Remove any air from the bag, seal and refrigerate for at least 2–3 hours.

. . . .

Cutting the lotus root into a flower shape is optional. Lotus root in round ring slices can also be used.

The sweetness and contrasting sourness become more prominent the next day.

PICKLED CHERRY TOMATO

8 cherry tomatoes

VINEGAR MIXTURE

2 Tbsp rice vinegar

4 Tbsp lemon juice

2 Tbsp olive oil

1 Tbsp raw sugar

Sea salt, as needed

At the base of the cherry tomatoes, make a small X-shaped cut. Add tomatoes into a pot of boiling water briefly for 15 seconds. Remove and shock the tomatoes in ice water. Gently peel the skin when cooled.

Whisk all the ingredients for the vinegar mixture together.

Put peeled tomatoes together with the vinegar mixture in a resealable bag. Remove any air from the bag, seal and refrigerate for at least 2 hours or overnight.

. . . .

You can substitute the cherry tomato with grape tomato.

Desserts

Traditionally, only seasonal fruits are served in *shojin ryori* meals. However, I find it interesting and elegant to prepare a dessert to complete the dining experience. The recipes in this section are simple, refreshing and vegan.

CHESTNUT WAGASHI

Serves 4

15-20 chestnuts, about 250 g (9 oz)

A pinch of sea salt

2 Tbsp raw sugar

Rinse the chestnuts. Pierce the chestnuts with a fork and steam it on medium heat for 30 minutes or until soft. Cut the steamed chestnuts into halves. Spoon out the flesh and place in a *suribachi*, or mortar and pestle.

Add sugar and salt and finely mash the chestnut. Press mashed chestnut through a fine sieve into a smooth paste. Divide chestnut paste into 8 portions and roll into balls.

Place each chestnut ball on a sheet of plastic wrap or muslin cloth and twist to wrap and shape. Unwrap and toast the top of each portion with a torch (this step is optional).

Arrange the chestnut *wagashi* on 4 individual plates and serve.

. . . .

A good test to eliminate spoiled chestnuts is to float them. Those that sink to the bottom are the good ones.

If the chestnut paste is too dry, add a small amount of water.

ORANGE JELLY

Serves 4

4 medium oranges

Kanten powder, 1 g per
100 ml (3¹/₃ fl oz) juice

Cut the tops off the oranges and carefully scoop out all
the flesh without breaking the skin, to get 4 orange cups.

Remove all the seeds (if any) from the flesh and cut into
chunks. Blend the orange chunks with a food processor
and pour the juice through a strainer to remove pulp.

Mix *kanten* powder with 2–3 tsp orange juice to form
a paste.

Pour 100 ml (3¹/₃ fl oz) orange juice in a saucepan and
bring to a boil. Remove from heat. Stir in *kanten* mixture,
followed by remaining juice.

Pour mixture into the orange cups and refrigerate for
1 hour or until the jelly is set. Cut the orange jelly into
wedges (with the orange skin) and arrange on
4 individual serving plates.

Pick the best-looking orange to make the orange cups.

Add raw sugar if the orange mixture is too sour.

You need a stand or small bowl to hold the orange cups
upright in the refrigerator while the jelly sets.

Try to gauge the volume required to fill the orange cups and
compensate the difference with water (if needed).

SOYMILK JELLY with STRAWBERRY

Serves 4

3 g ($^1/_{10}$ oz) *kanten* powder

300 ml (10 fl oz) soymilk (unsweetened)

6 strawberries

Mix *kanten* powder with 5 tsp soymilk to form a paste.

Heat rest of soymilk in a saucepan over low heat. Stir in the *kanten* mixture. Bring to a boil and immediately remove from heat. Set aside to cool for 10 minutes.

Pluck out the green tops from every strawberry and remove any green or white part. Cut the strawberry into halves lengthwise and arrange them neatly in a 17.5 x 8 x 6-cm (7 x 3 x 2$^1/_3$-in) metal tray.

Gently pour in the soymilk mixture. Refrigerate for about 1 hour or until the jelly is set.

Cut soymilk jelly into blocks and arrange on 4 individual plates to serve.

. . . .

The sweetness of this dish comes from the strawberries. Some strawberries may be a bit sour, so if desired, you can add raw sugar to the soymilk to sweeten it to taste.

SOYMILK MOUSSE

Serves 4

50 ml (1³/₄ fl oz) soymilk (unsweetened)

130 g (4¹/₂ oz) silken tofu

1 Tbsp raw sugar

1 Tbsp maple syrup

50 g (1³/₄ oz) banana

SUGAR SYRUP

30 g (1 oz) raw sugar

20 ml (²/₃ fl oz) water

To prepare the sugar syrup, combine sugar and water in a saucepan over low heat. Gently stir until all sugar is dissolved. Set aside to cool.

Add all ingredients (soymilk, tofu, banana, sugar and maple syrup) in a blender. Blend until smooth. Divide into 4 portions and keep refrigerated for about 2 hours.

To serve, add sugar syrup.

. . . .

The mousse can also be served topped with fruits or nuts.

SWEET POTATO CAKE

Serves 4

250 g (9 oz) Japanese sweet potatoes

100 g (3¹/₂ oz) banana

100 ml (3¹/₃ fl oz) soymilk (unsweetened)

4 g (¹/₁₀ oz) *kanten* powder

1 Tbsp black sesame seeds

Wash and cut sweet potatoes into rounds. Add sweet potatoes into a pot of boiling water, then simmer for 10–20 minutes or until tender. Drain and set aside to cool before peeling the skin.

Mix *kanten* powder with 2 Tbsp water to form a paste.

Add all the ingredients in a blender. Blend until smooth. Heat it up briefy in a pan for about 1 minute, stirring gently.

Transfer to a 17.5 x 8 x 6-cm (7 x 3 x 2¹/₃-in) metal tray and level smoothly with a spatula. Keep refrigerated for about 2 hours.

To serve, cut into blocks and arrange on 4 individual serving plates.

If it is not sweet enough, add raw sugar to the soymilk mixture to sweeten it to taste.

Glossary

Fresh Ingredients

01 Bamboo Shoot

This is the tender young shoot of the bamboo plant and it is usually available in spring and early summer. More work is required to prepare fresh bamboo shoot, but canned or vacuum-packed bamboo shoot are now easily available. These cream coloured shoots are commonly used in Asian cooking and enjoyed for their crunchy texture and mild, sweet flavour. Bamboo groves are common in the Zen temples and as such, the use of bamboo shoot in *shojin* cooking is a natural use of this food resource.

02 Burdock (Gobo)

Burdock is a root that is said to have many health benefits. It turns dark quickly when cut and as such, soak the cut burdock in water to prevent discolouration. This will also help remove any bitterness from the root. Choose burdock that is firm. To store, wrap in wet paper towels and place in a plastic bag in the refrigerator.

03 Chestnut

Known as *kuri* in Japanese, chestnuts are a favourite autumn food in Japan. Chestnuts have prickly husks and a double-layered shell protecting soft yellow flesh. Normally the prickly husk would have already been removed when you find them in the market. A good test to eliminate spoiled chestnuts is to float them. Those that sink to the bottom are the good ones.

04 Daikon

Daikon, also known as white radish, is a member of the radish family and the white-coloured root is especially large and succulent during winter. Although the leaves are edible, they turn yellow quite easily and are often removed when daikon is sold in stores. Daikon is known to aid digestion and promote respiratory health. It is widely used in Japanese cuisine.

05 Edamame

Edamame beans are soybeans that are still green and unripe in their pods. They are in season from summer to early autumn. Boiled edamame beans are commonly available as a side dish in Japanese restaurants, enjoyed for their light, sweet flavour. Fresh or frozen edamame beans are easily available from supermarkets.

06 Green Shiso

Green shiso or perilla is generally cultivated for use all year round. It is also known as Japanese basil, as it has a remarkable fragrance. It is often used as a garnish in sashimi dishes, or in salads and tempura.

07 Japanese Cucumber

Although cucumber season is in summer, cucumbers are now available all year round. The Japanese cucumber is less watery and has a firmer texture than regular cucumbers. It is also generally shorter and more slender compared with other varieties. The Japanese cucumber is enjoyed for its crunchy texture and sweet flavour.

08 Japanese Eggplant (Nasu)

There are many different varieties of eggplant, but the Japanese eggplant or *nasu* is usually sweeter than the others. Japanese eggplant has deep purple-coloured skin and firm flesh and is usually about 10–15-cm (4–6-in) long. Choose Japanese eggplant with a firm and shiny appearance and no obvious blemishes.

01

02

03

04

05

06

07

08

09 Japanese Pumpkin

A member of the squash family, the Japanese pumpkin or *kabocha* is slightly sweeter than other varieties of squash. It has rich yellow-coloured flesh and dark green skin. The skin of the pumpkin is edible except that it may be a bit tough if too thick. If so, thin the skin by peeling with a vegetable peeler.

10 Japanese Sweet Potato

Japanese sweet potato or *satsumaimo* season is in autumn. These tuberous roots have purplish red skin and whitish yellow flesh. Although largely similar to other types of sweet potato, Japanese sweet potatoes are sweeter and have a softer texture. Good quality Japanese sweet potatoes do not discolour easily when cut.

11 Lotus Root

Lotus root or *renkon* is typically harvested in winter. The root is characterised by air chambers that run through its length and create a pretty flower-like pattern when sliced crosswise. Choose lotus root that is thick, beige-white in colour and without blemishes.

12 Mountain Yams

Nagaimo and *yamatoimo* are different types of mountain yam tubers belonging to the Dioscorea family. Both *nagaimo* and *yamatoimo* are cylindrical in shape except that *yamatoimo* is fan-shaped at one end. *Nagaimo* is crunchy and more watery while *yamatoimo* has a dense and powdery texture. When selecting either yam, choose those that have a smooth, flawless surface without any bruises. To store, wrap in wet paper towels and place in a plastic bag in the refrigerator. Those with sensitive skin may experience itchiness when handling these yams. Wear gloves to avoid this and soothe any affected areas with vinegar or lemon juice.

13 Mushrooms, Eringi

Eringi mushrooms, also known as King Oyster, King Trumpet, French horn or Pleurotus Eryngii, has a thick, meaty white stem and small tan cap. Eringi has a high antioxidant content and is rich in nutrients. When cooked, it has an umami flavour with a texture similar to that of abalone. It is a popular part of the vegetarian diet.

14 Mushrooms, Shiitake

Shiitake mushrooms are cultivated edible fungi which are easily available on market shelves worldwide. The mushroom is famous for its rich texture and smoky flavour, and can be found in both fresh and dried forms. When buying fresh shiitake mushrooms, choose mushrooms that are firm and thick; the underside of the cap should be whitish.

15 Mushrooms, Shimeji

Shimeji mushrooms grow in clusters and have short, plump and spongy stems with brown caps. They cannot be eaten raw and must be cooked for their texture to become smooth with a firm bite. Choose shimeji mushrooms that are firm and plump.

16 Satoimo (Taro)

Satoimo or Japanese taro is a thickened underground stem called corm that is used by plants to store nutrients. It has hairy brown skin which needs to be peeled. *Taro* has a slippery texture, is low in calories and full of dietary fibre. It is cooked and eaten, typically, much like a potato. Like other varieties of *taro*, *satoimo* contains toxic calcium oxalate which can irritate the mouth and throat. However, this irritant is removed when cooked. Choose *taro* that is firm, heavy and unblemished.

17 Shungiku (Chrysanthemum Leaves)

Part of the chrysanthemum family, these greens are enjoyed as a vegetable in Japan. The *shungiku* is similar to another vegetable, *tong hao*, which is commonly used when serving steamboat in Asia. Compared to *tong hao*, Japanese *shungiku* has a more defined leaf pattern and a stronger fragrance. It is best eaten raw or very lightly cooked.

18 Shishito Pepper

Shishito are Japanese green peppers which are like green chili peppers. It is getting popular and can be found year-round though the growing season is in summer. Its mild sweetness makes it a great companion to many dishes.

Tofu

Tofu is made by coagulating soy milk and moulding the resulting curd into blocks. As it is rich in protein, tofu plays an important part in the vegetarian diet. There are several varieties of tofu and a few are used in the recipes in this book.

19 Abura-age

Abura-age is a deep fried tofu pocket or skin. It is made by deep frying thin slices of tofu, during which an air pocket naturally forms. *Abura-age* is popularly stuffed, but it can also be sliced and added to soups and stir-fries.

20 Atsuage

Atsuage is a thick, deep fried tofu. Large blocks of fresh tofu are deep fried until golden brown, giving the *atsuage* a crisp coating, while the tofu remains soft and smooth inside.

21 Momen Tofu

Momen tofu is also known as regular tofu. It has a firm texture that makes it easy to be picked up using chopsticks. In making *momen* tofu, cotton cloth is used to drain the curd, leaving a distinctive mark of the fabric on the blocks of tofu.

22 Silken Tofu

Silken tofu has a fine and delicate texture. It is produced by coagulating soy milk without curdling it. Traditionally, in Japanese cuisine, silken tofu is cut into delicate cubes to display the culinary knife skill of the chef. However, in *shojin* cooking, silken tofu is sometimes crumbled into pieces to express equanimity.

23 Umezuke (Pickled Plum)

Umeboshi, or *umezuke*, are salty and sour preserved plums (ume), a type of fruit closely related to the apricot. *Umeboshi* literally means dried ume. *Umezuke* indicates pickled ume which aren't dried (which is used in this cookbook). This pickled plum is said to have many beneficial effects on health such as reducing liver damage, supporting digestion and even blocking cancer cell growth.

24 Yuba

Yuba is a thin skin that is formed on the surface of boiled soymilk. It is high in protein and generally sold in fresh or dried sheets. The fresh *yuba* sheets are not as easily available as the dried ones, which need to be reconstituted by wetting quickly in water.

25 Yurine (Lily Bulb)

Yurine, the edible bulb of certain lily plants, is available during autumn in Japan and China. Outside of these countries, *yurine* is mostly found in packets although fresh *yurine*, imported from Japan, may sometimes be available. The creamy white bulbs separate into multiple petal-like segments when cut. *Yurine* has a mild, sweet flavour and a crunchy texture.

26 Yuzu

Yuzu is a citrus fruit with a delightful fragrance. It is usually available during late autumn and winter. *Yuzu* is rarely eaten as a fruit. Its rind is grated or sliced to garnish dishes and its juice is commonly used for seasoning. Lemon or lime peel can be used as substitutes if *yuzu* is not available.

Dry Ingredients

01 Barley
Barley is a healthy cereal grain which is high in fibre and protein while boasting numerous other health benefits. When cooked, it is chewy and has a nutty flavour. Barley is commonly available in packets which will indicate the cooking instructions or cooking time.

02 Dried Shiitake Mushroom
Dried shiitake mushrooms are important in shojin *cooking* for stocks and boiled dishes. Generally they are reconstituted in water until soft before use (see page 16).

03 Hijiki
Hijiki is a dark-coloured seaweed that is high in vitamins and minerals. It is said that the regular consumption of *hijiki* can contribute to a full head of dark, lustrous hair. Dried *hijiki* is sold in packet form and is widely available in Asian food stores. Rinse *hijiki* well to remove dirt, then reconstitute in water before use.

04 Kanten
Kanten is made from tengusa seaweed that is high in fibre and contains zero calories. It is used for its gelling properties and is an excellent option for vegetarians who do not use animal gelatin. *Kanten* is available in stick and powder form.

05 Karashi Powder
Karashi is Japanese yellow mustard made from powdered mustard seeds. A popular spicy condiment that is sold in either powder or paste form. Prepare *karashi* in powder form by mixing with lukewarm water to form a paste.

06 Katakuriko
Katakuriko is a starch originally derived from *katakuri* roots. However, it is commonly made from sweet potatoes or potatoes today due to the scarcity of *katakuri* roots. It can be used as a gluten-free substitute for plain (all-purpose) flour and as a thickening agent.

07 Konbu
Konbu is a type of seaweed and essential to Japanese cooking. It is rich in amino acids, iodine and calcium and is widely used to make stock. When choosing konbu, choose pieces that are thick and broad. Wipe the surface with a clean, damp cloth before using. Do not wash, as the white powder on the seaweed is the natural salt that contributes to the flavour.

08 Konnyaku
Konnyaku is a firm jelly made from the root of the devil's tongue. It has little taste of its own and is enjoyed mainly for its texture. *Konnyaku* is high in fibre and rich in minerals, and is consumed as a therapeutic food by Buddhist monks in Japan. *Konnyaku* is now also widely used in Japanese cooking.

09 Koyadofu
Koyadofu is freeze dried tofu and has other names such as *kori-dofu*, *shimi-dofu* and *kogori-dofu*. *Koyadofu* got its name from Mount Koya where winter can be extremely cold and the tofu got frozen. That is how *koyadofu* was first invented. It is now sold in blocks or cubes and can be preserved for a long time. Reconstitute *koyadofu* by soaking in water for a few minutes until it swells and become spongy. Then gently squeeze out excess moisture before using.

10 Kuromame (Black Soybeans)

Kuromame literally means black soybean and it is often served as one of the items in *osechi ryori*, traditional new year cuisine. "Mame" also means health and serving kuromame symbolises wishes for good health in the coming new year. *Kuromame* is also considered to be high in fibre and said to have many health benefits. It also has an appealing, shiny appearance.

11 Kuruma fu

Fu is made from gluten that is extracted from wheat flour and has wheat nutrients, excellent protein and zero fat; a good vegetable-derived protein source, especially in *shojin* cooking. *Kuruma fu* is shaped as flat large rings ("kuruma" in Japanese means wheel). It is normally reconstituted by soaking in water for a few minutes and then gently squeezing out excess moisture before using.

12 Kuzu

A member of the legume family, *kuzu* is known for its medicinal properties, especially for treating digestive ailments. The starch derived from the *kuzu* root gives food a good elasticity, and it is often used to make various types of "tofu" in *shojin* cooking.

13 Peanuts

Peanut (also known as groundnut or goober) is a legume grown mainly for its edible seeds. It is similar to walnut and almond, and commonly used in Western cuisines. The recipe in this cookbook uses peanuts that are already roasted and chopped.

14 Sesame Seeds

Both black and white sesame seeds are commonly used in Japanese cooking. These tiny teardrop-shape seeds are rich in nutrients, protein and minerals. Sesame seeds have a distinctive nutty aroma when toasted and ground.

15 Wakame

Wakame, is a sea vegetable or edible seaweed that is sold in fresh, salt-preserved and dried forms. Fresh wakame may be hard to find outside of Japan. Salt-preserved wakame needs to be rinsed free of salt and soaked in water for about 5 minutes. Dried wakame should be reconstituted by soaking in water for about 10 minutes until soft and fully expanded. Wakame has a sweet flavour and is most often served in soups and salads.

16 Wolfberry

Wolfberry, or goji, is used in traditional Chinese medicine and in food dishes in China. Wolfberry is divided into two sub-species, lycium barbarum and lycium chinense, both belonging to the Solanaceae family. It has medicinal properties that boosts our immune system and its functions.

Oils, Sauces and Condiments

01 Maple Syrup

Maple syrup is a syrup made from harvesting the sap of the maple tree. Though a Western product, it is commonly used in desserts and confectionary in Japan for its sweetness and fragrance. It is a good substitute for honey which cannot be used in *shojin* cuisine.

02 Mirin

Mirin is made from distilled sake mixed with rice malt and glutinous rice. It has a faint sake aroma and a refined sweetness. It is commonly used as a seasoning in Japanese cooking which gives the food a mild sweetness and a shiny glaze.

03 Miso, Sweet

Sweet miso, as the name suggests, is sweet due to a shorter fermentation time. The main ingredients used in making sweet miso are rice, barley and small amounts of soybeans.

04 Miso, Red and White

Miso is a fermented soybean paste widely used in Japanese cooking. Typically, miso can be categorised into two types: white miso and red miso. White miso is less salty and has a milder flavour compared to red miso. Within these two categories, there are many types of miso, depending on the region of origin and the ingredients used. For *shojin* cuisine, the miso should be made without bonito or other animal products.

05 Rice Vinegar

Rice vinegar is made from fermented rice or sake lees. It has a mild, sweet taste that is ideal for *shojin* cuisine. Rice vinegar is typically used to flavour Japanese rice used for making sushi. A few drops added to soaking liquid can also prevent food from discolouring.

06 Sake

Sake is a Japanese wine made from fermented rice. It is commonly used in Japanese cooking as

a seasoning to enhance the flavour of the food. Although Buddhist monks abstain from taking alcohol, the conservative amount of sake used in *shojin* cooking is negligible. If your cooked rice seems hard, add a few drops of sake for a softer texture. The sake will also add a mild sweetness and shine to the rice.

07 Sesame Oil

Sesame oil is derived from sesame seeds. It has a distinctive fragrance and a slightly sweet, nutty taste. Add a little sesame oil to dishes or dressings to enhance the flavour.

08 Soy Sauce

Soy sauce or *shoyu* is made from fermenting soybeans. There are many types of soy sauces available and the kind used in the recipes in this book is regular Japanese soy sauce. Select a brand that you like, but remember to use only Japanese soy sauce in Japanese cooking as Chinese soy sauce is different.

09 Wasabi

Wasabi, also known as Japanese horseradish, is a plant belonging to the same family as horseradish and mustard. Wasabi is sharp and pungent, and it is often served as a condiment to go with sushi or sashimi. Fresh wasabi is rare and expensive, even in Japan. If fresh wasabi is not available, wasabi paste or powder is a common substitute. In *shojin* cooking, use the powdered form as the paste may contain diary products.

10 White Sesame Paste

This is a thick, cream-coloured paste made from ground white sesame seeds and similar to tahini, which can be a substitute. Black sesame paste is also a commonly used ingredient in Japanese cooking.

11 Yuzu kosho

Yuzu kosho is a type of Japanese seasoning made from yuzu citrus peel, chili peppers and salt. It is an intensely fragrant and spicy condiment used in small quantities to zest up dishes. Though it can be more easily found in Japanese supermarkets, you should be able to find it online.

Weights & Measures

Quantities for this book are given in Metric, Imperial and American (spoon) measures. Standard spoon and cup measurements used are: 1 tsp = 5 ml, 1 Tbsp = 15 ml, 1 cup = 250 ml. All measures are level unless otherwise stated.

LIQUID AND VOLUME MEASURES

Metric	Imperial	American
5 ml	1/6 fl oz	1 teaspoon
10 ml	1/3 fl oz	1 dessertspoon
15 ml	1/2 fl oz	1 tablespoon
60 ml	2 fl oz	1/4 cup (4 tablespoons)
85 ml	2 1/2 fl oz	1/3 cup
90 ml	3 fl oz	3/8 cup (6 tablespoons)
125 ml	4 fl oz	1/2 cup
180 ml	6 fl oz	3/4 cup
250 ml	8 fl oz	1 cup
300 ml	10 fl oz (1/2 pint)	1 1/4 cups
375 ml	12 fl oz	1 1/2 cups
435 ml	14 fl oz	1 3/4 cups
500 ml	16 fl oz	2 cups
625 ml	20 fl oz (1 pint)	2 1/2 cups
750 ml	24 fl oz (1 1/5 pints)	3 cups
1 litre	32 fl oz (1 3/5 pints)	4 cups
1.25 litres	40 fl oz (2 pints)	5 cups
1.5 litres	48 fl oz (2 2/5 pints)	6 cups
2.5 litres	80 fl oz (4 pints)	10 cups

DRY MEASURES

Metric	Imperial
30 grams	1 ounce
45 grams	1 1/2 ounces
55 grams	2 ounces
70 grams	2 1/2 ounces
85 grams	3 ounces
100 grams	3 1/2 ounces
110 grams	4 ounces
125 grams	4 1/2 ounces
140 grams	5 ounces
280 grams	10 ounces
450 grams	16 ounces (1 pound)
500 grams	1 pound, 1 1/2 ounces
700 grams	1 1/2 pounds
800 grams	1 3/4 pounds
1 kilogram	2 pounds, 3 ounces
1.5 kilograms	3 pounds, 4 1/2 ounces
2 kilograms	4 pounds, 6 ounces

OVEN TEMPERATURE

	°C	°F	Gas Regulo
Very slow	120	250	1
Slow	150	300	2
Moderately slow	160	325	3
Moderate	180	350	4
Moderately hot	190/200	370/400	5/6
Hot	210/220	410/440	6/7
Very hot	230	450	8
Super hot	250/290	475/550	9/10

LENGTH

Metric	Imperial
0.5 cm	1/4 inch
1 cm	1/2 inch
1.5 cm	3/4 inch
2.5 cm	1 inch

Photographer: Liu Hongde

Published by Marshall Cavendish Cuisine
An imprint of Marshall Cavendish International

A member of the
Times Publishing Group

Other Marshall Cavendish Offices:
Marshall Cavendish Corporation, 800 Westchester Ave, Suite N-641,
Rye Brook, NY 10573, USA • Marshall Cavendish International (Thailand)
Co Ltd, 253 Asoke, 16th Floor, Sukhumvit 21 Road, Klongtoey Nua,
Wattana, Bangkok 10110, Thailand • Marshall Cavendish (Malaysia)
Sdn Bhd, Times Subang, Lot 46, Subang Hi-Tech Industrial Park,
Batu Tiga, 40000 Shah Alam, Selangor Darul Ehsan, Malaysia

National Library Board, Singapore Cataloguing in Publication Data

Name(s): Chu, Danny.
Title: Living shojin ryori : plant-based cooking from the heart / Danny Chu.
Description: Singapore : Marshall Cavendish Cuisine, [2021]
Identifier(s): OCN 1251469858 | ISBN 978-981-4974-85-1 (paperback)
Subject(s): LCSH: Cooking, Japanese. | Vegetarian cooking. | LCGFT:
Cookbooks.
Classification: DDC 641.5952--dc23

Printed in Singapore